To Be a Kid

Maya Ajmera and John D. Ivanko

NATIONAL GEOGRAPHIC Hampton-Brown

When you are a kid, you spend time with your family.

Portugal

Canada

Nepal

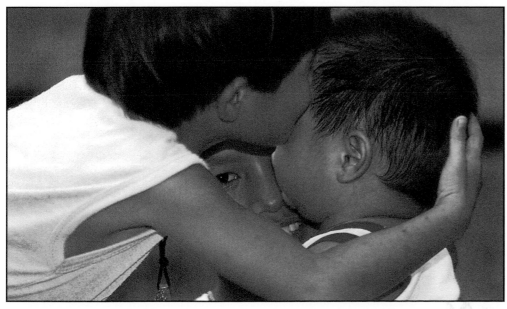

Philippines

Israel

3

Senegal

You go places

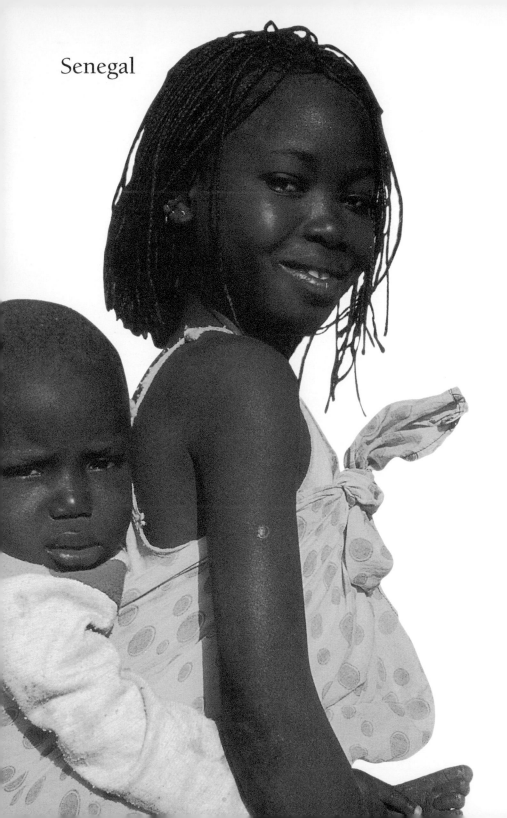

Nepal

with people who love you.

Japan

United States

You go to school

South Africa

Pakistan

Russia

and learn lots of new things.

Philippines

Ethiopia

Marshall Islands

7

You walk home together,

South Africa

share a story,

Guatemala

Ecuador

9

have a cool snack on a summer day,

Denmark   Bolivia

or march in a parade.

United States

Botswana

Ecuador

11

you play ball,

India

Cuba

Mexico

Antigua and Barbuda

run races,

Mexico

France

14

go skating,

Switzerland

Sweden

ride a merry-go-round,

Austria

or play a board game.

Nepal

France

United States

You paint beautiful pictures,

Poland

South Africa

share the joy
of music,

Peru

China

Ireland

or dance your
heart out.

Philippines

India

United States

United
Kingdom

21

You take care of animals.

United States

Japan

India

Haiti

Mongolia

Ecuador

23

You goof off

Madagascar

South Africa

and act silly.

Swaziland

Guatemala

Belize

25

When you are a kid, you make friends

Benin

China

Australia

26

that last forever and ever.

Oman

Mozambique

United States